Preface

Microsoft Azure Data Engineer DP 203: Data Engineering on Microsoft Azure is a meticulously structured guide designed to equip data professionals with the expertise required to design, implement, and manage data solutions within the Azure ecosystem. As organizations increasingly rely on data-driven decision-making, the demand for skilled data engineers capable of integrating, transforming, and securing vast amounts of structured and unstructured data has never been higher. This book serves as a comprehensive resource, aligned with the DP-203 certification objectives, covering essential topics such as data storage, processing, security, and optimization. By providing a structured approach to data engineering principles and best practices, this guide ensures that candidates develop a deep understanding of Azure's data services, enabling them to architect scalable, secure, and efficient analytics solutions.

Beyond exam preparation, Microsoft Certification DP-203: Data Engineering on Microsoft Azure emphasizes hands-on learning through practical exercises, real-world scenarios, and self-assessment tools designed to reinforce conceptual knowledge and technical proficiency. Each chapter integrates review questions, online test papers, and expert-led video tutorials to enhance learning and retention. Whether you are a beginner looking to establish a strong foundation in Azure data engineering or an experienced professional aiming to refine your skills and attain certification, this book provides a structured and comprehensive pathway to mastering the core competencies required for success in modern data engineering. We invite you to embark on this journey with us, gaining the knowledge and expertise needed to excel in the ever-evolving world of Azure data engineering.

Table of Contents

Chapter 1: Practice Questions & Answers Part 1

QUESTION 1
You need to ensure that the Twitter feed data can be analyzed in the dedicated SQL pool. The solution must meet the customer sentiment analytics requirements.
Which three Transaction-SQL DDL commands should you run in sequence? To answer, move the appropriate commands from the list of commands to the answer
area and arrange them in the correct order.
NOTE: More than one order of answer choices is correct. You will receive credit for any of the correct orders you select.
A. Mastered
B. Not Mastered
Answer: A

QUESTION 2
You need to implement an Azure Synapse Analytics database object for storing the sales transactions data. The solution must meet the sales transaction dataset
requirements.
What solution must meet the sales transaction dataset requirements.
What should you do? To answer, select the appropriate options in the answer area. NOTE: Each correct selection is worth one point.
A. Mastered
B. Not Mastered
Answer: A

QUESTION 3
- (Exam Topic 3)
You have several Azure Data Factory pipelines that contain a mix of the following types of activities.
Wrangling data flow
Notebook
Copy
Jar
Which two Azure services should you use to debug the activities? Each correct answer presents part of the solution NOTE: Each correct selection is worth one
point.
A. Azure HDInsight
B. Azure Databricks
C. Azure Machine Learning
D. Azure Data Factory
E. Azure Synapse Analytics
Answer: CE

QUESTION 4
- (Exam Topic 3)

You have files and folders in Azure Data Lake Storage Gen2 for an Azure Synapse workspace as shown in the following exhibit.
You create an external table named Ext Table that has LOCATION='/top folder/'.
When you query Ext Table by using an Azure Synapse Analytics serverless SQL pool, which files are returned?
A. File2.csv and File3.csv only
B. File1.csv and File4.csv only
C. File1.csv, File2.csv, File3.csv, and File4.csv
D. File1.csv only
Answer: C

QUESTION 5
- (Exam Topic 3)
You are monitoring an Azure Stream Analytics job.
The Backlogged Input Events count has been 20 for the last hour. You need to reduce the Backlogged Input Events count.
What should you do?
A. Drop late arriving events from the job.
B. Add an Azure Storage account to the job.
C. Increase the streaming units for the job.
D. Stop the job.
Answer: C

QUESTION 6
- (Exam Topic 3)
You use Azure Data Factory to prepare data to be queried by Azure Synapse Analytics serverless SQL pools. Files are initially ingested into an Azure Data Lake
Storage Gen2 account as 10 small JSON files. Each file contains the same data attributes and data from a subsidiary of your company.
You need to move the files to a different folder and transform the data to meet the following requirements: Provide the fastest possible query times.
Automatically infer the schema from the underlying files.
How should you configure the Data Factory copy activity? To answer, select the appropriate options in the answer area.
NOTE: Each correct selection is worth one point.

A. Mastered
B. Not Mastered
Answer: A

QUESTION 7
- (Exam Topic 3)
You need to schedule an Azure Data Factory pipeline to execute when a new file arrives in an Azure Data Lake Storage Gen2 container.
Which type of trigger should you use?
A. on-demand

B. tumbling window
C. schedule
D. event
Answer: D

QUESTION 8
- (Exam Topic 3)
What should you recommend using to secure sensitive customer contact information?
A. data labels
B. column-level security
C. row-level security
D. Transparent Data Encryption (TDE)
Answer: B

QUESTION 9
- (Exam Topic 3)
You have a Microsoft SQL Server database that uses a third normal form schema.
You plan to migrate the data in the database to a star schema in an A? \Ire Synapse Analytics dedicated SQI pool.
You need to design the dimension tables. The solution must optimize read operations.
What should you include in the solution? to answer, select the appropriate options in the answer area. NOTE: Each correct selection is worth one point.
A. Mastered
B. Not Mastered
Answer: A

QUESTION 10
- (Exam Topic 3)
You are designing a statistical analysis solution that will use custom proprietary1 Python functions on near real-time data from Azure Event Hubs.
You need to recommend which Azure service to use to perform the statistical analysis. The solution must minimize latency.
What should you recommend?
A. Azure Stream Analytics
B. Azure SQL Database
C. Azure Databricks
D. Azure Synapse Analytics
Answer: A

QUESTION 10
- (Exam Topic 3)
You are designing a real-time dashboard solution that will visualize streaming data from remote sensors that connect to the internet. The streaming data must be
aggregated to show the average value of each 10-second interval. The data will be discarded after being displayed in the dashboard.
The solution will use Azure Stream Analytics and must meet the following requirements:

Minimize latency from an Azure Event hub to the dashboard.
Minimize the required storage.
Minimize development effort.
What should you include in the solution? To answer, select the appropriate options in the answer area. NOTE: Each correct selection is worth one point
A. Mastered
B. Not Mastered
Answer: A

QUESTION 11
- (Exam Topic 3)
You have an Azure SQL database named Database1 and two Azure event hubs named HubA and Hub. The data consumed from each source is shown in the following table.
You need to implement Azure Stream Analytics to calculate the average fare per mile by driver.
How should you configure the Stream Analytics input for each source? To answer, select the appropriate options in the answer area.
NOTE: Each correct selection is worth one point.
A. Mastered
B. Not Mastered
Answer: A

QUESTION 12
- (Exam Topic 3)
Note: This question is part of a series of questions that present the same scenario. Each question in the series contains a unique solution that might meet the stated goals. Some question sets might have more than one correct solution, while others might not have a correct solution.
After you answer a question in this section, you will NOT be able to return to it. As a result, these questions will not appear in the review screen.
You are designing an Azure Stream Analytics solution that will analyze Twitter data.
You need to count the tweets in each 10-second window. The solution must ensure that each tweet is counted only once.
Does this meet the goal?
A. Yes
B. No
Answer: A

QUESTION 13
- (Exam Topic 3)
You have an Azure subscription that contains the following resources:
* An Azure Active Directory (Azure AD) tenant that contains a security group named Group1.
* An Azure Synapse Analytics SQL pool named Pool1.
You need to control the access of Group1 to specific columns and rows in a table in Pool1
Which Transact-SQL commands should you use? To answer, select the appropriate options in the answer area. NOTE: Each appropriate options in the answer

area.
A. Mastered
B. Not Mastered
Answer: A
QUESTION 14
- (Exam Topic 3)
You plan to implement an Azure Data Lake Gen2 storage account.
You need to ensure that the data lake will remain available if a data center fails in the primary Azure region. The solution must minimize costs.
Which type of replication should you use for the storage account?
A. geo-redundant storage (GRS)
B. zone-redundant storage (ZRS)
C. locally-redundant storage (LRS)
D. geo-zone-redundant storage (GZRS)
Answer: A

QUESTION 15
- (Exam Topic 3)
You have an Azure subscription that contains a logical Microsoft SQL server named Server1. Server1 hosts an Azure Synapse Analytics SQL dedicated pool
named Pool1.
You need to recommend a Transparent Data Encryption (TDE) solution for Server1. The solution must meet the following requirements:
 Track the usage of encryption keys.
 Maintain the access of client apps to Pool1 in the event of an Azure datacenter outage that affects the availability of the encryption keys.

What should you include in the recommendation? To answer, select the appropriate options in the answer area.
NOTE: Each correct selection is worth one point.
A. Mastered
B. Not Mastered
Answer: A

QUESTION 16
- (Exam Topic 3)
You are designing an application that will store petabytes of medical imaging data
When the data is first created, the data will be accessed frequently during the first week. After one month, the data must be accessible within 30 seconds, but files
will be accessed infrequently. After one year, the data will be accessed infrequently but must be accessible within five minutes.
You need to select a storage strategy for the data. The solution must minimize costs.
Which storage tier should you use for each time frame? To answer, select the appropriate options in the answer area.
NOTE: Each correct selection is worth one point.
A. Mastered

B. Not Mastered
Answer: A

QUESTION 17
- (Exam Topic 3)
You plan to create an Azure Synapse Analytics dedicated SQL pool.
You need to minimize the time it takes to identify queries that return confidential information as defined by the company's data privacy regulations and the users
who executed the queues.
Which two components should you include in the solution? Each correct answer presents part of the solution. NOTE: Each correct selection is worth one point.
A. sensitivity-classification labels applied to columns that contain confidential information
B. resource tags for databases that contain confidential information
C. audit logs sent to a Log Analytics workspace
D. dynamic data masking for columns that contain confidential information
Answer: AC

QUESTION 18
- (Exam Topic 3)
You are designing an Azure Databricks table. The table will ingest an average of 20 million streaming events per day.
You need to persist the events in the table for use in incremental load pipeline jobs in Azure Databricks. The solution must minimize storage costs and incremental load times.
What should you include in the solution?
A. Partition by Date Time fields.
B. Sink to Azure Queue storage.
C. Include a watermark column.
D. Use a JSON format for physical data storage.
Answer: B

QUESTION 19
- (Exam Topic 3)
You need to implement an Azure Databricks cluster that automatically connects to Azure Data Lake Storage Gen2 by using Azure Active Directory (Azure AD)
integration.
How should you configure the new cluster? To answer, select the appropriate options in the answer area. NOTE: Each correct selection is worth one point.
A. Mastered
B. Not Mastered
Answer: A

QUESTION 20
- (Exam Topic 3)
You implement an enterprise data warehouse in Azure Synapse Analytics. You have a large fact table that is 10 terabytes (TB) in size.

Incoming queries use the primary key SaleKey column to retrieve data as displayed in the following table:
You need to distribute the large fact table across multiple nodes to optimize performance of the table. Which technology should you use?
A. hash distributed table with clustered index
B. hash distributed table with clustered Columnstore index
C. round robin distributed table with clustered index
D. round robin distributed table with clustered Columnstore index
E. heap table with distribution replicate
Answer: B

QUESTION 21
- (Exam Topic 3)
You have an Azure Stream Analytics job that is a Stream Analytics project solution in Microsoft Visual Studio. The job accepts data generated by IoT devices in the
JSON format.
You need to modify the job to accept data generated by the IoT devices in the Protobuf format.
Which three actions should you perform from Visual Studio on sequence? To answer, move the appropriate actions from the list of actions to the answer area and
arrange them in the correct order.
A. Mastered
B. Not Mastered
Answer: A

QUESTION 22
- (Exam Topic 3)
You have an Azure data factory.
You need to ensure that pipeline-run data is retained for 120 days. The solution must ensure that you can query the data by using the Kusto query language.
Which four actions should you perform in sequence? To answer, move the appropriate actions from the list of actions to the answer area and arrange them in the
correct order.
NOTE: More than one order of answer choices is correct. You will receive credit for any of the correct orders you select.
A. Mastered
B. Not Mastered
Answer: A
QUESTION 23
- (Exam Topic 3)
You are designing an inventory updates table in an Azure Synapse Analytics dedicated SQL pool. The table will have a clustered columnstore index and will
include the following columns:
- EventDate: 1 million per day
- EventTypelD: 10 million per event type
- WarehouselD: 100 million per warehouse

• ProductCategoryTypeiD: 25 million per product category type You identify the following usage patterns:
Analyst will most commonly analyze transactions for a warehouse.
Queries will summarize by product category type, date, and/or inventory event type. You need to recommend a partition strategy for the table to minimize query
times. On which column should you recommend partitioning the table?
A. ProductCategoryTypeID
B. EventDate
C. WarehouseID
D. EventTypeID
Answer: D

QUESTION 24
- (Exam Topic 3)
You are creating dimensions for a data warehouse in an Azure Synapse Analytics dedicated SQL pool. You create a table by using the Transact-SQL statement
shown in the following exhibit.
Use the drop-down menus to select the answer choice that completes each statement based on the information presented in the graphic.
NOTE: Each correct selection is worth one point.
A. Mastered
B. Not Mastered
Answer: A

QUESTION 25
- (Exam Topic 3)
You are designing a fact table named FactPurchase in an Azure Synapse Analytics dedicated SQL pool. The table contains purchases from suppliers for a retail
store. FactPurchase will contain the following columns.
FactPurchase will have 1 million rows of data added daily and will contain three years of data. Transact-SQL queries similar to the following query will be executed
daily.

```
SELECT
SupplierKey, StockItemKey, COUNT(*)
FROM FactPurchase
WHERE DateKey >= 20210101
AND DateKey <= 20210131
GROUP By SupplierKey, StockItemKey
```

Which table distribution will minimize query times?
A. round-robin
B. replicated
C. hash-distributed on DateKey
D. hash-distributed on PurchaseKey
Answer: D

QUESTION 26

- (Exam Topic 3)
You are planning a streaming data solution that will use Azure Databricks. The solution will stream sales transaction data from an online store. The solution has
the following specifications:
* The output data will contain items purchased, quantity, line total sales amount, and line total tax amount.
* Line total sales amount and line total tax amount will be aggregated in Databricks.
* Sales transactions will never be updated. Instead, new rows will be added to adjust a sale.
You need to recommend an output mode for the dataset that will be processed by using Structured Streaming. The solution must minimize duplicate data.
What should you recommend?
A. Append
B. Update
C. Complete
Answer: C

QUESTION 27
- (Exam Topic 3)
You need to output files from Azure Data Factory.
Which file format should you use for each type of output? To answer, select the appropriate options in the answer area.
NOTE: Each correct selection is worth one point.
A. Mastered
B. Not Mastered
Answer: A

QUESTION 28
- (Exam Topic 3)
You have the following table named Employees.
You need to calculate the employee _type value based on the hire date value.
How should you complete the Transact-SQL statement? To answer, drag the appropriate values to the correct targets. Each value may be used once, more than
once, or not at all. You may need to drag the split bar between panes or scroll to view content
NOTE: Each correct selection is worth one point.
A. Mastered
B. Not Mastered
Answer: A

QUESTION 29
- (Exam Topic 3)
You use Azure Data Lake Storage Gen2.
You need to ensure that workloads can use filter predicates and column projections to filter data at the time the data is read from disk.
Which two actions should you perform? Each correct answer presents part of the solution. NOTE: Each correct selection is worth one point.
A. Reregister the Microsoft Data Lake Store resource provider.

B. Reregister the Azure Storage resource provider.
C. Create a storage policy that is scoped to a container.
D. Register the query acceleration feature.
E. Create a storage policy that is scoped to a container prefix filter.
Answer: BD

QUESTION 30
- (Exam Topic 3)
You create an Azure Databricks cluster and specify an additional library to install. When you attempt to load the library to a notebook, the library in not found.
You need to identify the cause of the issue. What should you review?
A. notebook logs
B. cluster event logs
C. global init scripts logs
D. workspace logs
Answer: C

QUESTION 31
- (Exam Topic 3)
You have an Azure Stream Analytics query. The query returns a result set that contains 10,000 distinct values for a column named clusterID.
You monitor the Stream Analytics job and discover high latency. You need to reduce the latency.
Which two actions should you perform? Each correct answer presents a complete solution. NOTE: Each correct selection is worth one point.
A. Add a pass-through query.
B. Add a temporal analytic function.
C. Scale out the query by using PARTITION BY.
D. Convert the query to a reference query.
E. Increase the number of streaming units.
Answer: CE

QUESTION 32
- (Exam Topic 3)
You have an Azure Storage account and a data warehouse in Azure Synapse Analytics in the UK South region. You need to copy blob data from the storage
account to the data warehouse by using Azure Data Factory. The solution must meet the following requirements:
 Ensure that the data remains in the UK South region at all times.
 Minimize administrative effort.
Which type of integration runtime should you use?
A. Azure integration runtime
B. Azure-SSIS integration runtime
C. Self-hosted integration runtime
Answer: A

QUESTION 33

- (Exam Topic 3)
You have an Azure Stream Analytics job that receives clickstream data from an Azure event hub. You need to define a query in the Stream Analytics job. The query must meet the following requirements: Count the number of clicks within each 10-second
window based on the country of a visitor.
Ensure that each click is NOT counted more than once. How should you define the Query?
A. SELECT Country, Avg(*) AS AverageFROM ClickStream TIMESTAMP BY CreatedAt GROUP BY Country, SlidingWindow(second, 10)
B. SELECT Country, Count(*) AS CountFROM ClickStream TIMESTAMP BY CreatedAt GROUP BY Country, TumblingWindow(second, 10)
C. SELECT Country, Avg(*) AS AverageFROM ClickStream TIMESTAMP BY CreatedAt GROUP BY Country, HoppingWindow(second, 10, 2)
D. SELECT Country, Count(*) AS CountFROM ClickStream TIMESTAMP BY CreatedAt GROUP BY Country, SessionWindow(second, 5, 10)
Answer: B

QUESTION 34
- (Exam Topic 3)
You develop data engineering solutions for a company.
A project requires the deployment of data to Azure Data Lake Storage.
You need to implement role-based access control (RBAC) so that project members can manage the Azure Data Lake Storage resources.
Which three actions should you perform? Each correct answer presents part of the solution. NOTE: Each correct selection is worth one point.
A. Assign Azure AD security groups to Azure Data Lake Storage.
B. Configure end-user authentication for the Azure Data Lake Storage account.
C. Configure service-to-service authentication for the Azure Data Lake Storage account.
D. Create security groups in Azure Active Directory (Azure AD) and add project members.
E. Configure access control lists (ACL) for the Azure Data Lake Storage account.
Answer: ADE

QUESTION 35
- (Exam Topic 3)
You have a data model that you plan to implement in a data warehouse in Azure Synapse Analytics as shown in the following exhibit.
All the dimension tables will be less than 2 GB after compression, and the fact table will be approximately 6 TB.
Which type of table should you use for each table?
A. Mastered
B. Not Mastered
Answer: A

QUESTION 36
- (Exam Topic 3)
You have an Azure Data Lake Storage Gen2 container that contains 100 TB of data.

You need to ensure that the data in the container is available for read workloads in a secondary region if an outage occurs in the primary region. The solution must minimize costs.

Which type of data redundancy should you use?

A. zone-redundant storage (ZRS)

B. read-access geo-redundant storage (RA-GRS)

C. locally-redundant storage (LRS)

D. geo-redundant storage (GRS)

Answer: C

QUESTION 37

- (Exam Topic 3)

You plan to implement an Azure Data Lake Storage Gen2 container that will contain CSV files. The size of the files will vary based on the number of events that occur per hour.

File sizes range from 4.KB to 5 GB.

You need to ensure that the files stored in the container are optimized for batch processing. What should you do?

A. Compress the files.

B. Merge the files.

C. Convert the files to JSON

D. Convert the files to Avro.

Answer: D

QUESTION 38

- (Exam Topic 3)

You need to design an Azure Synapse Analytics dedicated SQL pool that meets the following requirements:

 Can return an employee record from a given point in time.

 Maintains the latest employee information.

 Minimizes query complexity.

How should you model the employee data?

A. as a temporal table

B. as a SQL graph table

C. as a degenerate dimension table

D. as a Type 2 slowly changing dimension (SCD) table

Answer: D

QUESTION 39

- (Exam Topic 3)

You are designing an Azure Stream Analytics solution that receives instant messaging data from an Azure event hub.

You need to ensure that the output from the Stream Analytics job counts the number of messages per time zone every 15 seconds.

How should you complete the Stream Analytics query? To answer, select the appropriate options in the answer area.
NOTE: Each correct selection is worth one point.
A. Mastered
B. Not Mastered
Answer: A

QUESTION 40
- (Exam Topic 3)
Note: This question is part of a series of questions that present the same scenario. Each question in the series contains a unique solution that might meet the
stated goals. Some question sets might have more than one correct solution, while others might not have a correct solution.
After you answer a question in this section, you will NOT be able to return to it. As a result, these questions will not appear in the review screen.
You are designing an Azure Stream Analytics solution that will analyze Twitter data.
You need to count the tweets in each 10-second window. The solution must ensure that each tweet is counted only once.
Solution: You use a session window that uses a timeout size of 10 seconds. Does this meet the goal?
A. Yes
B. No
Answer: B

QUESTION 41
You need to ensure that the Twitter feed data can be analyzed in the dedicated SQL pool. The solution must meet the customer sentiment analytics requirements.
Which three Transaction-SQL DDL commands should you run in sequence? To answer, move the appropriate commands from the list of commands to the answer
area and arrange them in the correct order.
NOTE: More than one order of answer choices is correct. You will receive credit for any of the correct orders you select.
A. Mastered
B. Not Mastered
Answer: A

QUESTION 42
You need to implement an Azure Synapse Analytics database object for storing the sales transactions data. The solution must meet the sales transaction dataset
requirements.
What solution must meet the sales transaction dataset requirements.
What should you do? To answer, select the appropriate options in the answer area. NOTE: Each correct selection is worth one point.
A. Mastered
B. Not Mastered
Answer: A

QUESTION 43
- (Exam Topic 3)
You have several Azure Data Factory pipelines that contain a mix of the following types of activities.
* Wrangling data flow
* Notebook
* Copy
* jar
Which two Azure services should you use to debug the activities? Each correct answer presents part of the solution NOTE: Each correct selection is worth one
point.
A. Azure HDInsight
B. Azure Databricks
C. Azure Machine Learning
D. Azure Data Factory
E. Azure Synapse Analytics
Answer: CE

QUESTION 44
- (Exam Topic 3)
You have files and folders in Azure Data Lake Storage Gen2 for an Azure Synapse workspace as shown in the following exhibit.
You create an external table named ExtTable that has LOCATION='/topfolder/'.
When you query ExtTable by using an Azure Synapse Analytics serverless SQL pool, which files are returned?
A. File2.csv and File3.csv only
B. File1.csv and File4.csv only
C. File1.csv, File2.csv, File3.csv, and File4.csv
D. File1.csv only
Answer: C

QUESTION 45
- (Exam Topic 3)
You are monitoring an Azure Stream Analytics job.
The Backlogged Input Events count has been 20 for the last hour. You need to reduce the Backlogged Input Events count.
What should you do?
A. Drop late arriving events from the job.
B. Add an Azure Storage account to the job.
C. Increase the streaming units for the job.
D. Stop the job.
Answer: C

QUESTION 46
- (Exam Topic 3)

You use Azure Data Factory to prepare data to be queried by Azure Synapse Analytics serverless SQL pools. Files are initially ingested into an Azure Data Lake
Storage Gen2 account as 10 small JSON files. Each file contains the same data attributes and data from a subsidiary of your company.
You need to move the files to a different folder and transform the data to meet the following requirements: Provide the fastest possible query times.
Automatically infer the schema from the underlying files.
How should you configure the Data Factory copy activity? To answer, select the appropriate options in the answer area.
NOTE: Each correct selection is worth one point.
A. Mastered
B. Not Mastered
Answer: A

QUESTION 47
- (Exam Topic 3)
You need to schedule an Azure Data Factory pipeline to execute when a new file arrives in an Azure Data Lake Storage Gen2 container.
Which type of trigger should you use?
A. on-demand
B. tumbling window
C. schedule
D. event
Answer: D

QUESTION 48
- (Exam Topic 3)
What should you recommend using to secure sensitive customer contact information?
A. data labels
B. column-level security
C. row-level security
D. Transparent Data Encryption (TDE)
Answer: B

QUESTION 49
- (Exam Topic 3)
You have a Microsoft SQL Server database that uses a third normal form schema.
You plan to migrate the data in the database to a star schema in an A?\ire Synapse Analytics dedicated SQI pool.
You need to design the dimension tables. The solution must optimize read operations.
What should you include in the solution? to answer, select the appropriate options in the answer area. NOTE: Each correct selection is worth one point.
A. Mastered
B. Not Mastered
Answer: A
QUESTION 50

- (Exam Topic 3)
You are designing a statistical analysis solution that will use custom proprietary1 Python functions on near real-time data from Azure Event Hubs.
You need to recommend which Azure service to use to perform the statistical analysis. The solution must minimize latency.
What should you recommend?
A. Azure Stream Analytics
B. Azure SQL Database
C. Azure Databricks
D. Azure Synapse Analytics
Answer: A

QUESTION 51
- (Exam Topic 3)
You are designing a real-time dashboard solution that will visualize streaming data from remote sensors that connect to the internet. The streaming data must be
aggregated to show the average value of each 10-second interval. The data will be discarded after being displayed in the dashboard.
The solution will use Azure Stream Analytics and must meet the following requirements:
Minimize latency from an Azure Event hub to the dashboard.
Minimize the required storage.
Minimize development effort.
What should you include in the solution? To answer, select the appropriate options in the answer area. NOTE: Each correct selection is worth one point
A. Mastered
B. Not Mastered
Answer: A

QUESTION 52
- (Exam Topic 3)
You have an Azure SQL database named Database1 and two Azure event hubs named HubA and HubB. The data consumed from each source is shown in the
following table.
You need to implement Azure Stream Analytics to calculate the average fare per mile by driver.
How should you configure the Stream Analytics input for each source? To answer, select the appropriate options in the answer area.
NOTE: Each correct selection is worth one point.
A. Mastered
B. Not Mastered
Answer: A

QUESTION 53
- (Exam Topic 3)
Note: This question is part of a series of questions that present the same scenario. Each question in the series contains a unique solution that might meet the

stated goals. Some question sets might have more than one correct solution, while others might not have a correct solution.
After you answer a question in this section, you will NOT be able to return to it. As a result, these questions will not appear in the review screen.
You are designing an Azure Stream Analytics solution that will analyze Twitter data.
You need to count the tweets in each 10-second window. The solution must ensure that each tweet is counted only once.
Does this meet the goal?
A. Yes
B. No
Answer: A

QUESTION 54
- (Exam Topic 3)
You have an Azure subscription that contains the following resources:
* An Azure Active Directory (Azure AD) tenant that contains a security group named Group1.
* An Azure Synapse Analytics SQL pool named Pool1.
You need to control the access of Group1 to specific columns and rows in a table in Pool1
Which Transact-SQL commands should you use? To answer, select the appropriate options in the answer area. NOTE: Each appropriate options in the answer
area.
A. Mastered
B. Not Mastered
Answer: A

QUESTION 55
- (Exam Topic 3)
You plan to implement an Azure Data Lake Gen2 storage account.
You need to ensure that the data lake will remain available if a data center fails in the primary Azure region. The solution must minimize costs.
Which type of replication should you use for the storage account?
A. geo-redundant storage (GRS)
B. zone-redundant storage (ZRS)
C. locally-redundant storage (LRS)
D. geo-zone-redundant storage (GZRS)
Answer: A

QUESTION 56
- (Exam Topic 3)
You have an Azure subscription that contains a logical Microsoft SQL server named Server1. Server1 hosts an Azure Synapse Analytics SQL dedicated pool
named Pool1.
You need to recommend a Transparent Data Encryption (TDE) solution for Server1. The solution must meet the following requirements:
Track the usage of encryption keys.

Maintain the access of client apps to Pool1 in the event of an Azure datacenter outage that affects the availability of the encryption keys.
What should you include in the recommendation? To answer, select the appropriate options in the answer area.
NOTE: Each correct selection is worth one point.
A. Mastered
B. Not Mastered
Answer: A

QUESTION 57
- (Exam Topic 3)
You are designing an application that will store petabytes of medical imaging data
When the data is first created, the data will be accessed frequently during the first week. After one month, the data must be accessible within 30 seconds, but files
will be accessed infrequently. After one year, the data will be accessed infrequently but must be accessible within five minutes.
You need to select a storage strategy for the data. The solution must minimize costs.
Which storage tier should you use for each time frame? To answer, select the appropriate options in the answer area.
NOTE: Each correct selection is worth one point.
A. Mastered
B. Not Mastered
Answer: A

QUESTION 58
- (Exam Topic 3)
You plan to create an Azure Synapse Analytics dedicated SQL pool.
You need to minimize the time it takes to identify queries that return confidential information as defined by the company's data privacy regulations and the users
who executed the queues.
Which two components should you include in the solution? Each correct answer presents part of the solution. NOTE: Each correct selection is worth one point.
A. sensitivity-classification labels applied to columns that contain confidential information
B. resource tags for databases that contain confidential information
C. audit logs sent to a Log Analytics workspace
D. dynamic data masking for columns that contain confidential information
Answer: AC

QUESTION 59
- (Exam Topic 3)
You are designing an Azure Databricks table. The table will ingest an average of 20 million streaming events per day.
You need to persist the events in the table for use in incremental load pipeline jobs in Azure Databricks. The solution must minimize storage costs and incremental load times.
What should you include in the solution?
A. Partition by DateTime fields.

B. Sink to Azure Queue storage.
C. Include a watermark column.
D. Use a JSON format for physical data storage.
Answer: B

QUESTION 60
- (Exam Topic 3)
You need to implement an Azure Databricks cluster that automatically connects to Azure Data Lake Storage Gen2 by using Azure Active Directory (Azure AD)
integration.
How should you configure the new cluster? To answer, select the appropriate options in the answer area. NOTE: Each correct selection is worth one point.
A. Mastered
B. Not Mastered
Answer: A

QUESTION 61
- (Exam Topic 3)
You implement an enterprise data warehouse in Azure Synapse Analytics. You have a large fact table that is 10 terabytes (TB) in size.
Incoming queries use the primary key SaleKey column to retrieve data as displayed in the following table:
You need to distribute the large fact table across multiple nodes to optimize performance of the table. Which technology should you use?
A. hash distributed table with clustered index
B. hash distributed table with clustered Columnstore index
C. round robin distributed table with clustered index
D. round robin distributed table with clustered Columnstore index
E. heap table with distribution replicate
Answer: B

QUESTION 62
- (Exam Topic 3)
You have an Azure Stream Analytics job that is a Stream Analytics project solution in Microsoft Visual Studio. The job accepts data generated by IoT devices in the
JSON format.
You need to modify the job to accept data generated by the IoT devices in the Protobuf format.
Which three actions should you perform from Visual Studio on sequence? To answer, move the appropriate actions from the list of actions to the answer area and
arrange them in the correct order.
A. Mastered
B. Not Mastered

QUESTION 63
- (Exam Topic 3)
You have an Azure data factory.

You need to ensure that pipeline-run data is retained for 120 days. The solution must ensure that you can query the data by using the Kusto query language.
Which four actions should you perform in sequence? To answer, move the appropriate actions from the list of actions to the answer area and arrange them in the
correct order.
NOTE: More than one order of answer choices is correct. You will receive credit for any of the correct orders you select.
A. Mastered
B. Not Mastered
Answer: A

QUESTION 64
- (Exam Topic 3)
You are designing an inventory updates table in an Azure Synapse Analytics dedicated SQL pool. The table will have a clustered columnstore index and will
include the following columns:
• EventDate: 1 million per day
• EventTypelD: 10 million per event type
• WarehouselD: 100 million per warehouse
• ProductCategoryTypeiD: 25 million per product category type You identify the following usage patterns:
Analyst will most commonly analyze transactions for a warehouse.
Queries will summarize by product category type, date, and/or inventory event type. You need to recommend a partition strategy for the table to minimize query
times. On which column should you recommend partitioning the table?
A. ProductCategoryTypeID
B. EventDate
C. WarehouseID
D. EventTypeID
Answer: D

QUESTION 65
- (Exam Topic 3)
You are creating dimensions for a data warehouse in an Azure Synapse Analytics dedicated SQL pool. You create a table by using the Transact-SQL statement
shown in the following exhibit.
Use the drop-down menus to select the answer choice that completes each statement based on the information presented in the graphic.
NOTE: Each correct selection is worth one point.
A. Mastered
B. Not Mastered
Answer: A

QUESTION 66
- (Exam Topic 3)

You are designing a fact table named FactPurchase in an Azure Synapse Analytics dedicated SQL pool. The table contains purchases from suppliers for a retail
store. FactPurchase will contain the following columns.
FactPurchase will have 1 million rows of data added daily and will contain three years of data. Transact-SQL queries similar to the following query will be executed
daily.

```
SELECT
SupplierKey, StockItemKey, COUNT(*)
FROM FactPurchase
WHERE DateKey >= 20210101
AND DateKey <= 20210131
GROUP By SupplierKey, StockItemKey
```

Which table distribution will minimize query times?
A. round-robin
B. replicated
C. hash-distributed on DateKey
D. hash-distributed on PurchaseKey
Answer: D
QUESTION 67
- (Exam Topic 3)
You are planning a streaming data solution that will use Azure Databricks. The solution will stream sales transaction data from an online store. The solution has
the following specifications:
* The output data will contain items purchased, quantity, line total sales amount, and line total tax amount.
* Line total sales amount and line total tax amount will be aggregated in Databricks.
* Sales transactions will never be updated. Instead, new rows will be added to adjust a sale.
You need to recommend an output mode for the dataset that will be processed by using Structured Streaming. The solution must minimize duplicate data.
What should you recommend?
A. Append
B. Update
C. Complete
Answer: C

QUESTION 68
- (Exam Topic 3)
You need to output files from Azure Data Factory.
Which file format should you use for each type of output? To answer, select the appropriate options in the answer area.
NOTE: Each correct selection is worth one point.
A. Mastered
B. Not Mastered
Answer: A

QUESTION 69

- (Exam Topic 3)
You have the following table named Employees.
You need to calculate the employee _type value based on the hire date value.
How should you complete the Transact-SQL statement? To answer, drag the appropriate values to the correct targets. Each value may be used once, more than
once, or not at all. You may need to drag the split bar between panes or scroll to view content
NOTE: Each correct selection is worth one point.
A. Mastered
B. Not Mastered
Answer: A

QUESTION 70
- (Exam Topic 3)
You use Azure Data Lake Storage Gen2.
You need to ensure that workloads can use filter predicates and column projections to filter data at the time the data is read from disk.
Which two actions should you perform? Each correct answer presents part of the solution. NOTE: Each correct selection is worth one point.
A. Reregister the Microsoft Data Lake Store resource provider.
B. Reregister the Azure Storage resource provider.
C. Create a storage policy that is scoped to a container.
D. Register the query acceleration feature.
E. Create a storage policy that is scoped to a container prefix filter.
Answer: BD

QUESTION 71
- (Exam Topic 3)
You create an Azure Databricks cluster and specify an additional library to install. When you attempt to load the library to a notebook, the library in not found.
You need to identify the cause of the issue. What should you review?
A. notebook logs
B. cluster event logs
C. global init scripts logs
D. workspace logs
Answer: C

QUESTION 72
- (Exam Topic 3)
You have an Azure Stream Analytics query. The query returns a result set that contains 10,000 distinct values for a column named clusterID.
You monitor the Stream Analytics job and discover high latency. You need to reduce the latency.
Which two actions should you perform? Each correct answer presents a complete solution. NOTE: Each correct selection is worth one point.
A. Add a pass-through query.
B. Add a temporal analytic function.
C. Scale out the query by using PARTITION BY.

D. Convert the query to a reference query.
E. Increase the number of streaming units.
Answer: CE

QUESTION 73
- (Exam Topic 3)
You have an Azure Storage account and a data warehouse in Azure Synapse Analytics in the UK South region. You need to copy blob data from the storage account to the data warehouse by using Azure Data Factory. The solution must meet the following requirements:
Ensure that the data remains in the UK South region at all times.
Minimize administrative effort.
Which type of integration runtime should you use?
A. Azure integration runtime
B. Azure-SSIS integration runtime
C. Self-hosted integration runtime
Answer: A

QUESTION 74
- (Exam Topic 3)
You have an Azure Stream Analytics job that receives clickstream data from an Azure event hub. You need to define a query in the Stream Analytics job. The query must meet the following requirements: Count the number of clicks within each 10-second window based on the country of a visitor.
Ensure that each click is NOT counted more than once. How should you define the Query?
A. SELECT Country, Avg(*) AS AverageFROM ClickStream TIMESTAMP BY CreatedAt GROUP BY Country, SlidingWindow(second, 10)
B. SELECT Country, Count(*) AS CountFROM ClickStream TIMESTAMP BY CreatedAt GROUP BY Country, TumblingWindow(second, 10)
C. SELECT Country, Avg(*) AS AverageFROM ClickStream TIMESTAMP BY CreatedAt GROUP BY Country, HoppingWindow(second, 10, 2)
D. SELECT Country, Count(*) AS CountFROM ClickStream TIMESTAMP BY CreatedAt GROUP BY Country, SessionWindow(second, 5, 10)
Answer: B

QUESTION 75
- (Exam Topic 3)
You develop data engineering solutions for a company.
A project requires the deployment of data to Azure Data Lake Storage.
You need to implement role-based access control (RBAC) so that project members can manage the Azure Data Lake Storage resources.
Which three actions should you perform? Each correct answer presents part of the solution. NOTE: Each correct selection is worth one point.
A. Assign Azure AD security groups to Azure Data Lake Storage.
B. Configure end-user authentication for the Azure Data Lake Storage account.
C. Configure service-to-service authentication for the Azure Data Lake Storage account.

D. Create security groups in Azure Active Directory (Azure AD) and add project members.
E. Configure access control lists (ACL) for the Azure Data Lake Storage account.
Answer: ADE

QUESTION 76
- (Exam Topic 3)
You have a data model that you plan to implement in a data warehouse in Azure Synapse Analytics as shown in the following exhibit.
All the dimension tables will be less than 2 GB after compression, and the fact table will be approximately 6 TB.
Which type of table should you use for each table? To answer, select the appropriate options in the answer area.
NOTE: Each correct selection is worth one point.
A. Mastered
B. Not Mastered
Answer: A

QUESTION 77
- (Exam Topic 3)
You have an Azure Data Lake Storage Gen2 container that contains 100 TB of data.
You need to ensure that the data in the container is available for read workloads in a secondary region if an outage occurs in the primary region. The solution must
minimize costs.
Which type of data redundancy should you use?
A. zone-redundant storage (ZRS)
B. read-access geo-redundant storage (RA-GRS)
C. locally-redundant storage (LRS)
D. geo-redundant storage (GRS)
Answer: C

QUESTION 78
- (Exam Topic 3)
You plan to implement an Azure Data Lake Storage Gen2 container that will contain CSV files. The size of the files will vary based on the number of events that
occur per hour.
File sizes range from 4.KB to 5 GB.
You need to ensure that the files stored in the container are optimized for batch processing. What should you do?
A. Compress the files.
B. Merge the files.
C. Convert the files to JSON
D. Convert the files to Avro.
Answer: D

QUESTION 79
- (Exam Topic 3)

You need to design an Azure Synapse Analytics dedicated SQL pool that meets the following requirements:
Can return an employee record from a given point in time.
Maintains the latest employee information.
Minimizes query complexity.
How should you model the employee data?
A. as a temporal table
B. as a SQL graph table
C. as a degenerate dimension table
D. as a Type 2 slowly changing dimension (SCD) table
Answer: D

QUESTION 80
- (Exam Topic 3)
You are designing an Azure Stream Analytics solution that receives instant messaging data from an Azure event hub.
You need to ensure that the output from the Stream Analytics job counts the number of messages per time
zone every 15 seconds.
How should you complete the Stream Analytics query? To answer, select the appropriate options in the answer area.
NOTE: Each correct selection is worth one point.
A. Mastered
B. Not Mastered
Answer: A

QUESTION 81
- (Exam Topic 3)
Note: This question is part of a series of questions that present the same scenario. Each question in the series contains a unique solution that might meet the
stated goals. Some question sets might have more than one correct solution, while others might not have a correct solution.
After you answer a question in this section, you will NOT be able to return to it. As a result, these questions will not appear in the review screen.
You are designing an Azure Stream Analytics solution that will analyze Twitter data.
You need to count the tweets in each 10-second window. The solution must ensure that each tweet is counted only once.
Solution: You use a session window that uses a timeout size of 10 seconds. Does this meet the goal?
A. Yes
B. No
Answer: B

QUESTION 82
You need to design a data storage structure for the product sales transactions. The solution must meet the sales transaction dataset requirements.

What should you include in the solution? To answer, select the appropriate options in the answer area. NOTE: Each correct selection is worth one point.
A. Mastered
B. Not Mastered
Answer: A

QUESTION 83
- (Exam Topic 3)
You need to collect application metrics, streaming query events, and application log messages for an Azure Databrick cluster.
Which type of library and workspace should you implement? To answer, select the appropriate options in the answer area.
NOTE: Each correct selection is worth one point.
A. Mastered
B. Not Mastered
Answer: A

QUESTION 84
- (Exam Topic 3)
You have an on-premises data warehouse that includes the following fact tables. Both tables have the following columns: DateKey, ProductKey, RegionKey. There
are 120 unique product keys and 65 unique region keys.
Queries that use the data warehouse take a long time to complete.
You plan to migrate the solution to use Azure Synapse Analytics. You need to ensure that the Azure-based solution optimizes query performance and minimizes
processing skew.
What should you recommend?
A. Mastered
B. Not Mastered
Answer: A

QUESTION 85
- (Exam Topic 3)
You have files and folders in Azure Data Lake Storage Gen2 for an Azure Synapse workspace as shown in the following exhibit.
You create an external table named ExtTable that has LOCATION='/topfolder/'.
When you query ExtTable by using an Azure Synapse Analytics serverless SQL pool, which files are returned?
A. File2.csv and File3.csv only
B. File1.csv and File4.csv only
C. File1.csv, File2.csv, File3.csv, and File4.csv
D. File1.csv only
Answer: C

QUESTION 86
- (Exam Topic 3)

You need to create an Azure Data Factory pipeline to process data for the following three departments at your company: Ecommerce, retail, and wholesale. The solution must ensure that data can also be processed for the entire company.
How should you complete the Data Factory data flow script? To answer, drag the appropriate values to the correct targets. Each value may be used once, more than once, or not at all. You may need to drag the split bar between panes or scroll to view content.
NOTE: Each correct selection is worth one point.
A. Mastered
B. Not Mastered
Answer: A

QUESTION 87
- (Exam Topic 3)
You are building an Azure Stream Analytics job to identify how much time a user spends interacting with a feature on a webpage.
The job receives events based on user actions on the webpage. Each row of data represents an event. Each event has a type of either 'start' or 'end'.
You need to calculate the duration between start and end events.
How should you complete the query? To answer, select the appropriate options in the answer area.
NOTE: Each correct selection is worth one point.
A. Mastered
B. Not Mastered
Answer: A

QUESTION 88
- (Exam Topic 3)
You have a self-hosted integration runtime in Azure Data Factory.
The current status of the integration runtime has the following configurations:
Status: Running
Type: Self-Hosted
Version: 4.4.7292.1
Running / Registered Node(s): 1/1
High Availability Enabled: False
Linked Count: 0
Queue Length: 0
Average Queue Duration. 0.00s
The integration runtime has the following node details:
Name: X-M
Status: Running
Version: 4.4.7292.1
Available Memory: 7697MB
CPU Utilization: 6%
Network (In/Out): 1.21KBps/0.83KBps
Concurrent Jobs (Running/Limit): 2/14
Role: Dispatcher/Worker
Credential Status: In Sync

Use the drop-down menus to select the answer choice that completes each statement based on the information presented.
A. Mastered
B. Not Mastered
Answer: A

QUESTION 89
- (Exam Topic 3)
You have an Apache Spark DataFrame named temperatures. A sample of the data is shown in the following table.
You need to produce the following table by using a Spark SQL query.
How should you complete the query? To answer, drag the appropriate values to the correct targets. Each value may be used once more than once, or not at all.
You may need to drag the split bar between panes or scroll to view content.
A. Mastered
B. Not Mastered
Answer: A

QUESTION 90
- (Exam Topic 3)
You have a C# application that process data from an Azure IoT hub and performs complex transformations. You need to replace the application with a real-time
solution. The solution must reuse as much code as possible from the existing application.
A. Azure Databricks
B. Azure Event Grid
C. Azure Stream Analytics
D. Azure Data Factory
Answer: C

QUESTION 91
- (Exam Topic 3)
You are developing a solution using a Lambda architecture on Microsoft Azure. The data at test layer must meet the following requirements:
Data storage:
•Serve as a repository (or high volumes of large files in various formats.
•Implement optimized storage for big data analytics workloads.
•Ensure that data can be organized using a hierarchical structure. Batch processing:
•Use a managed solution for in-memory computation processing.
•Natively support Scala, Python, and R programming languages.
•Provide the ability to resize and terminate the cluster automatically. Analytical data store:
•Support parallel processing.
•Use columnar storage.
•Support SQL-based languages.
You need to identify the correct technologies to build the Lambda architecture.
Which technologies should you use? To answer, select the appropriate options in the answer area NOTE: Each correct selection is worth one point.

A. Mastered
B. Not Mastered
Answer: A

QUESTION 92
- (Exam Topic 3)
You have an Azure Databricks workspace named workspace1 in the Standard pricing tier.
You need to configure workspace1 to support autoscaling all-purpose clusters. The solution must meet the following requirements:
Automatically scale down workers when the cluster is underutilized for three minutes.
Minimize the time it takes to scale to the maximum number of workers.
Minimize costs.
What should you do first?
A. Enable container services for workspace1.
B. Upgrade workspace1 to the Premium pricing tier.
C. Set Cluster Mode to High Concurrency.
D. Create a cluster policy in workspace1.
Answer: B

QUESTION 93
- (Exam Topic 3)
You are designing an Azure Databricks table. The table will ingest an average of 20 million streaming events per day.
You need to persist the events in the table for use in incremental load pipeline jobs in Azure Databricks. The solution must minimize storage costs and incremental
load times.
What should you include in the solution?
A. Partition by DateTime fields.
B. Sink to Azure Queue storage.
C. Include a watermark column.
D. Use a JSON format for physical data storage.
Answer: B

QUESTION 94
- (Exam Topic 3)
You have an Azure Synapse Analytics dedicated SQL pool that contains a large fact table. The table contains 50 columns and 5 billion rows and is a heap.
Most queries against the table aggregate values from approximately 100 million rows and return only two columns.
You discover that the queries against the fact table are very slow. Which type of index should you add to provide the fastest query times?
A. nonclustered columnstore
B. clustered columnstore
C. nonclustered
D. clustered
Answer: B

QUESTION 95

- (Exam Topic 3)

You implement an enterprise data warehouse in Azure Synapse Analytics. You have a large fact table that is 10 terabytes (TB) in size.

Incoming queries use the primary key SaleKey column to retrieve data as displayed in the following table:

You need to distribute the large fact table across multiple nodes to optimize performance of the table. Which technology should you use?

A. hash distributed table with clustered index

B. hash distributed table with clustered Columnstore index

C. round robin distributed table with clustered index

D. round robin distributed table with clustered Columnstore index

E. heap table with distribution replicate

Answer: B

QUESTION 96

- (Exam Topic 3)

You are designing an inventory updates table in an Azure Synapse Analytics dedicated SQL pool. The table will have a clustered columnstore index and will
include the following columns:

• EventDate: 1 million per day

• EventTypelD: 10 million per event type

• WarehouselD: 100 million per warehouse

• ProductCategoryTypeiD: 25 million per product category type You identify the following usage patterns:

Analyst will most commonly analyze transactions for a warehouse.

Queries will summarize by product category type, date, and/or inventory event type. You need to recommend a partition strategy for the table to minimize query
times. On which column should you recommend partitioning the table?

A. ProductCategoryTypeID

B. EventDate

C. WarehouseID

D. EventTypeID

Answer: D

QUESTION 97

- (Exam Topic 3)

You are creating dimensions for a data warehouse in an Azure Synapse Analytics dedicated SQL pool. You create a table by using the Transact-SQL statement
shown in the following exhibit.

Use the drop-down menus to select the answer choice that completes each statement based on the information presented in the graphic.

NOTE: Each correct selection is worth one point.

A. Mastered

B. Not Mastered

Answer: A

QUESTION 98

- (Exam Topic 3)

You have an Azure Stream Analytics query. The query returns a result set that contains 10,000 distinct values for a column named clusterID.

You monitor the Stream Analytics job and discover high latency. You need to reduce the latency.

Which two actions should you perform? Each correct answer presents a complete solution. NOTE: Each correct selection is worth one point.

A. Add a pass-through query.

B. Add a temporal analytic function.

C. Scale out the query by using PARTITION BY.

D. Convert the query to a reference query.

E. Increase the number of streaming units.

Answer: CE

QUESTION 99

- (Exam Topic 3)

You have an Azure Stream Analytics job that receives clickstream data from an Azure event hub.

You need to define a query in the Stream Analytics job. The query must meet the following requirements: Count the number of clicks within each 10-second window based on the country of a visitor.

Ensure that each click is NOT counted more than once. How should you define the Query?

A. SELECT Country, Avg(*) AS AverageFROM ClickStream TIMESTAMP BY CreatedAt GROUP BY Country, SlidingWindow(second, 10)

B. SELECT Country, Count(*) AS CountFROM ClickStream TIMESTAMP BY CreatedAt GROUP BY Country, TumblingWindow(second, 10)

C. SELECT Country, Avg(*) AS AverageFROM ClickStream TIMESTAMP BY CreatedAt GROUP BY Country, HoppingWindow(second, 10, 2)

D. SELECT Country, Count(*) AS CountFROM ClickStream TIMESTAMP BY CreatedAt GROUP BY Country, SessionWindow(second, 5, 10)

Answer: B

QUESTION 100

- (Exam Topic 3)

You have an Azure Data Lake Storage Gen2 container that contains 100 TB of data.

You need to ensure that the data in the container is available for read workloads in a secondary region if an outage occurs in the primary region. The solution must minimize costs.

Which type of data redundancy should you use?

A. zone-redundant storage (ZRS)

B. read-access geo-redundant storage (RA-GRS)

C. locally-redundant storage (LRS)

D. geo-redundant storage (GRS)

Answer: C

Chapter 2: Practice Questions & Answers Part 2

QUESTION 101

- (Exam Topic 3)

Note: This question is part of a series of questions that present the same scenario. Each question in the series contains a unique solution that might meet the stated goals. Some question sets might have more than one correct solution, while others might not have a correct solution.

After you answer a question in this section, you will NOT be able to return to it. As a result, these questions will not appear in the review screen.

You are designing an Azure Stream Analytics solution that will analyze Twitter data.

You need to count the tweets in each 10-second window. The solution must ensure that each tweet is counted only once.

Solution: You use a session window that uses a timeout size of 10 seconds. Does this meet the goal?

A. Yes

B. No

Answer: B

QUESTION 102

- (Exam Topic 3)

You have an Azure Synapse workspace named MyWorkspace that contains an Apache Spark database named mytestdb.

You run the following command in an Azure Synapse Analytics Spark pool in MyWorkspace.

CREATE TABLE mytestdb.myParquetTable(

EmployeeID int, EmployeeName string, EmployeeStartDate date) USING Parquet

You then use Spark to insert a row into mytestdb.myParquetTable. The row contains the following data.

One minute later, you execute the following query from a serverless SQL pool in MyWorkspace.

SELECT EmployeeID

FROM mytestdb.dbo.myParquetTable WHERE name = 'Alice';

What will be returned by the query?

A. 24

B. an error

C. a null value

Answer: A

QUESTION 103

- (Exam Topic 3)

You are designing a dimension table for a data warehouse. The table will track the value of the dimension attributes over time and preserve the history of the data by adding new rows as the data changes.

Which type of slowly changing dimension (SCD) should use?

A. Type 0

B. Type 1

C. Type 2

D. Type 3
Answer: C

QUESTION 104
- (Exam Topic 3)
You use Azure Stream Analytics to receive Twitter data from Azure Event Hubs and to output the data to an Azure Blob storage account.
You need to output the count of tweets during the last five minutes every five minutes. Each tweet must only be counted once.
Which windowing function should you use?
A. a five-minute Session window
B. a five-minute Sliding window
C. a five-minute Tumbling window
D. a five-minute Hopping window that has one-minute hop
Answer: C

QUESTION 105
You need to design the partitions for the product sales transactions. The solution must mee the sales transaction dataset requirements.
What should you include in the solution? To answer, select the appropriate options in the answer area. NOTE: Each correct selection is worth one point.
A. Mastered
B. Not Mastered
Answer: A

QUESTION 106
You need to integrate the on-premises data sources and Azure Synapse Analytics. The solution must meet the data integration requirements.
Which type of integration runtime should you use?
A. Azure-SSIS integration runtime
B. self-hosted integration runtime
C. Azure integration runtime
Answer: C

QUESTION 107
You need to implement an Azure Synapse Analytics database object for storing the sales transactions data. The solution must meet the sales transaction dataset
requirements.
What solution must meet the sales transaction dataset requirements.
What should you do? To answer, select the appropriate options in the answer area. NOTE: Each correct selection is worth one point.
A. Mastered
B. Not Mastered
Answer: A

QUESTION 108

- (Exam Topic 3)
You are designing a slowly changing dimension (SCD) for supplier data in an Azure Synapse Analytics dedicated SQL pool.
You plan to keep a record of changes to the available fields. The supplier data contains the following columns.
Which three additional columns should you add to the data to create a Type 2 SCD? Each correct answer presents part of the solution.
NOTE: Each correct selection is worth one point.
A. surrogate primary key
B. foreign key
C. effective start date
D. effective end date
E. last modified date
F. business key
Answer: BCF

QUESTION 109
- (Exam Topic 3)
You use Azure Data Factory to prepare data to be queried by Azure Synapse Analytics serverless SQL pools. Files are initially ingested into an Azure Data Lake
Storage Gen2 account as 10 small JSON files. Each file contains the same data attributes and data from a subsidiary of your company.
You need to move the files to a different folder and transform the data to meet the following requirements: Provide the fastest possible query times.
Automatically infer the schema from the underlying files.
How should you configure the Data Factory copy activity?
B. Not Mastered
Answer: A

QUESTION 110
- (Exam Topic 3)
You have an Azure Synapse Analytics dedicated SQL pool that contains a table named Table1.
You have files that are ingested and loaded into an Azure Data Lake Storage Gen2 container named container1.
You plan to insert data from the files into Table1 and azure Data Lake Storage Gen2 container named container1.
You plan to insert data from the files into Table1 and transform the data. Each row of data in the files will produce one row in the serving layer of Table1.
You need to ensure that when the source data files are loaded to container1, the DateTime is stored as an additional column in Table1.
Solution: You use a dedicated SQL pool to create an external table that has a additional DateTime column. Does this meet the goal?
A. Yes
B. No
Answer: A

QUESTION 111
- (Exam Topic 3)
You have a self-hosted integration runtime in Azure Data Factory.
The current status of the integration runtime has the following configurations:
Status: Running
Type: Self-Hosted
Version: 4.4.7292.1
Running / Registered Node(s): 1/1
High Availability Enabled: False
Linked Count: 0
Queue Length: 0
Average Queue Duration. 0.00s
The integration runtime has the following node details:
Name: X-M
Status: Running
Version: 4.4.7292.1
Available Memory: 7697MB
CPU Utilization: 6%
Network (In/Out): 1.21KBps/0.83KBps
Concurrent Jobs (Running/Limit): 2/14
Role: Dispatcher/Worker
Credential Status: In Sync
Use the drop-down menus to select the answer choice that completes each statement based on the information presented.
NOTE: Each correct selection is worth one point.
A. Mastered
B. Not Mastered
Answer: A

QUESTION 112
- (Exam Topic 3)
What should you recommend to prevent users outside the Litware on-premises network from accessing the analytical data store?
A. a server-level virtual network rule
B. a database-level virtual network rule
C. a database-level firewall IP rule
D. a server-level firewall IP rule
Answer: A

QUESTION 113
- (Exam Topic 3)
You are designing a solution that will copy Parquet files stored in an Azure Blob storage account to an Azure Data Lake Storage Gen2 account.
The data will be loaded daily to the data lake and will use a folder structure of {Year}/{Month}/{Day}/.

You need to design a daily Azure Data Factory data load to minimize the data transfer between the two accounts.
Which two configurations should you include in the design? Each correct answer presents part of the solution. NOTE: Each correct selection is worth one point.
A. Delete the files in the destination before loading new data.
B. Filter by the last modified date of the source files.
C. Delete the source files after they are copied.
D. Specify a file naming pattern for the destination.
Answer: BC

QUESTION 114
- (Exam Topic 3)
You plan to monitor an Azure data factory by using the Monitor & Manage app.
You need to identify the status and duration of activities that reference a table in a source database.
Which three actions should you perform in sequence? To answer, move the actions from the list of actions to the answer are and arrange them in the correct order.
A. Mastered
B. Not Mastered
Answer: A
QUESTION 115
- (Exam Topic 3)
You have an Azure Synapse Analytics serverless SQL pool named Pool1 and an Azure Data Lake Storage Gen2 account named storage1. The
AllowedBlobpublicAccess porperty is disabled for storage1.
You need to create an external data source that can be used by Azure Active Directory (Azure AD) users to access storage1 from Pool1.
What should you create first?
A. an external resource pool
B. a remote service binding
C. database scoped credentials
D. an external library
Answer: C

QUESTION 116
- (Exam Topic 3)
Note: This question is part of a series of questions that present the same scenario. Each question in the series contains a unique solution that might meet the
stated goals. Some question sets might have more than one correct solution, while others might not have a correct solution.
After you answer a question in this section, you will NOT be able to return to it. As a result, these questions will not appear in the review screen.
You plan to create an Azure Databricks workspace that has a tiered structure. The workspace will contain the following three workloads:
A workload for data engineers who will use Python and SQL.
A workload for jobs that will run notebooks that use Python, Scala, and SOL.
A workload that data scientists will use to perform ad hoc analysis in Scala and R.

The enterprise architecture team at your company identifies the following standards for Databricks environments:
The data engineers must share a cluster.
The job cluster will be managed by using a request process whereby data scientists and data engineers provide packaged notebooks for deployment to the cluster.
All the data scientists must be assigned their own cluster that terminates automatically after 120 minutes of inactivity. Currently, there are three data scientists.
You need to create the Databricks clusters for the workloads.
Solution: You create a Standard cluster for each data scientist, a High Concurrency cluster for the data engineers, and a High Concurrency cluster for the jobs.
Does this meet the goal?
A. Yes
B. No
Answer: A

QUESTION 117
- (Exam Topic 3)
You are designing an Azure Databricks table. The table will ingest an average of 20 million streaming events per day.
You need to persist the events in the table for use in incremental load pipeline jobs in Azure Databricks. The solution must minimize storage costs and incremental load times.
What should you include in the solution?
A. Partition by DateTime fields.
B. Sink to Azure Queue storage.
C. Include a watermark column.
D. Use a JSON format for physical data storage.
Answer: B

QUESTION 118
- (Exam Topic 3)
You have an Azure Synapse Analytics dedicated SQL pool that contains a large fact table. The table contains 50 columns and 5 billion rows and is a heap.
Most queries against the table aggregate values from approximately 100 million rows and return only two columns.
You discover that the queries against the fact table are very slow. Which type of index should you add to provide the fastest query times?
A. nonclustered columnstore
B. clustered columnstore
C. nonclustered
D. clustered
Answer: B

QUESTION 119
- (Exam Topic 3)

You have an Azure data factory.
You need to ensure that pipeline-run data is retained for 120 days. The solution must ensure that you can query the data by using the Kusto query language.
Which four actions should you perform in sequence?
B. Not Mastered
Answer: A

QUESTION 120
- (Exam Topic 3)
You are designing an enterprise data warehouse in Azure Synapse Analytics that will contain a table named Customers. Customers will contain credit card
information.
You need to recommend a solution to provide salespeople with the ability to view all the entries in Customers. The solution must prevent all the salespeople from
viewing or inferring the credit card information.
What should you include in the recommendation?
A. data masking
B. Always Encrypted
C. column-level security
D. row-level security
Answer: A

QUESTION 121
- (Exam Topic 3)
You are creating dimensions for a data warehouse in an Azure Synapse Analytics dedicated SQL pool. You create a table by using the Transact-SQL statement
shown in the following exhibit.
Use the drop-down menus to select the answer choice that completes each statement based on the information presented in the graphic.
NOTE: Each correct selection is worth one point.
A. Mastered
B. Not Mastered
Answer: A

QUESTION 122
- (Exam Topic 3)
Note: This question is part of a series of questions that present the same scenario. Each question in the series contains a unique solution that might meet the
stated goals. Some question sets might have more than one correct solution, while others might not have a correct solution.
After you answer a question in this scenario, you will NOT be able to return to it. As a result, these questions will not appear in the review screen.
You have an Azure Storage account that contains 100 GB of files. The files contain text and numerical values. 75% of the rows contain description data that has
an average length of 1.1 MB.

You plan to copy the data from the storage account to an Azure SQL data warehouse. You need to prepare the files to ensure that the data copies quickly.
Solution: You modify the files to ensure that each row is less than 1 MB. Does this meet the goal?
A. Yes
B. No
Answer: A

QUESTION 123
- (Exam Topic 3)
You have two Azure Data Factory instances named ADFdev and ADFprod. ADFdev connects to an Azure DevOps Git repository.
You publish changes from the main branch of the Git repository to ADFdev. You need to deploy the artifacts from ADFdev to ADFprod.
What should you do first?
A. From ADFdev, modify the Git configuration.
B. From ADFdev, create a linked service.
C. From Azure DevOps, create a release pipeline.
D. From Azure DevOps, update the main branch.
Answer: C

QUESTION 124
- (Exam Topic 3)
Note: This question is part of a series of questions that present the same scenario. Each question in the series contains a unique solution that might meet the
stated goals. Some question sets might have more than one correct solution, while others might not have a correct solution.
After you answer a question in this section, you will NOT be able to return to it. As a result, these questions will not appear in the review screen.
You are designing an Azure Stream Analytics solution that will analyze Twitter data.
You need to count the tweets in each 10-second window. The solution must ensure that each tweet is counted only once.
Solution: You use a hopping window that uses a hop size of 5 seconds and a window size 10 seconds. Does this meet the goal?
A. Yes
B. No
Answer: B

QUESTION 125
- (Exam Topic 3)
You are designing a sales transactions table in an Azure Synapse Analytics dedicated SQL pool. The table will contains approximately 60 million rows per month
and will be partitioned by month. The table will use a clustered column store index and round-robin distribution.
Approximately how many rows will there be for each combination of distribution and partition?
A. 1 million
B. 5 million

C. 20 million
D. 60 million
Answer: D

QUESTION 126
- (Exam Topic 3)
You have an Azure Stream Analytics query. The query returns a result set that contains 10,000 distinct values for a column named clusterID.
You monitor the Stream Analytics job and discover high latency. You need to reduce the latency. Which two actions should you perform? Each correct answer presents a complete solution. NOTE: Each correct selection is worth one point.
A. Add a pass-through query.
B. Add a temporal analytic function.
C. Scale out the query by using PARTITION BY.
D. Convert the query to a reference query.
E. Increase the number of streaming units.
Answer: CE

QUESTION 127
- (Exam Topic 3)
You are building an Azure Analytics query that will receive input data from Azure IoT Hub and write the results to Azure Blob storage.
You need to calculate the difference in readings per sensor per hour.
How should you complete the query? To answer, select the appropriate options in the answer area. NOTE: Each correct selection is worth one point.
A. Mastered
B. Not Mastered
Answer: A

QUESTION 128
- (Exam Topic 3)
You need to design an Azure Synapse Analytics dedicated SQL pool that meets the following requirements:
 Can return an employee record from a given point in time.
 Maintains the latest employee information.
 Minimizes query complexity.
How should you model the employee data?
A. as a temporal table
B. as a SQL graph table
C. as a degenerate dimension table
D. as a Type 2 slowly changing dimension (SCD) table
Answer: D

QUESTION 129
- (Exam Topic 3)
You are designing the folder structure for an Azure Data Lake Storage Gen2 container.

Users will query data by using a variety of services including Azure Databricks and Azure Synapse Analytics serverless SQL pools. The data will be secured by
subject area. Most queries will include data from the current year or current month.
Which folder structure should you recommend to support fast queries and simplified folder security?
A.
/{SubjectArea}/{DataSource}/{DD}/{MM}/{YYYY}/{FileData}_{YYYY}_{MM}_{DD}.csv
B.
/{DD}/{MM}/{YYYY}/{SubjectArea}/{DataSource}/{FileData}_{YYYY}_{MM}_{DD}.csv
C.
/{YYYY}/{MM}/{DD}/{SubjectArea}/{DataSource}/{FileData}_{YYYY}_{MM}_{DD}.csv
D.
/{SubjectArea}/{DataSource}/{YYYY}/{MM}/{DD}/{FileData}_{YYYY}_{MM}_{DD}.csv
Answer: D

QUESTION 130
- (Exam Topic 3)
You are designing an Azure Stream Analytics solution that receives instant messaging data from an Azure event hub.
You need to ensure that the output from the Stream Analytics job counts the number of messages per time
zone every 15 seconds.
How should you complete the Stream Analytics query? To answer, select the appropriate options in the answer area.
NOTE: Each correct selection is worth one point.
A. Mastered
B. Not Mastered
Answer: A

QUESTION 131
- (Exam Topic 3)
You plan to ingest streaming social media data by using Azure Stream Analytics. The data will be stored in files in Azure Data Lake Storage, and then consumed
by using Azure Datiabricks and PolyBase in Azure Synapse Analytics.
You need to recommend a Stream Analytics data output format to ensure that the queries from Databricks and PolyBase against the files encounter the fewest
possible errors. The solution must ensure that the tiles can be queried quickly and that the data type information is retained.
What should you recommend?
A. Parquet
B. Avro
C. CSV
D. JSON
Answer: B

QUESTION 132

- (Exam Topic 3)
You have an Azure Data Lake Storage Gen2 container.
Data is ingested into the container, and then transformed by a data integration application. The data is NOT modified after that. Users can read files in the
container but cannot modify the files.
You need to design a data archiving solution that meets the following requirements: New data is accessed frequently and must be available as quickly as
possible.
Data that is older than five years is accessed infrequently but must be available within one second when requested.
Data that is older than seven years is NOT accessed. After seven years, the data must be persisted at the lowest cost possible.
Costs must be minimized while maintaining the required availability.
How should you manage the data? To answer, select the appropriate options in the answer area.
NOTE: Each correct selection is worth one point
A. Mastered
B. Not Mastered
Answer: A

QUESTION 133
A company is planning on creating an Azure SQL database to support a mission critical application. The application needs to be highly available and not have any performance degradation during maintenance windows.
Which of the following technologies can be used to implement this solution?
(Choose 3)
a) Premium Service Tier
b) Virtual Machine Scale Sets
c) Basic Service Tier
d) SQL Data Sync
e) Always On Availability Groups
f) Zone-redundant configuration
Answer:a,e,f

QUESTION 134
02. A company has a SaaS solution that uses Azure SQL Database with elastic pools. The solution contains a dedicated database for each customer organization. Customer organizations have peak usage at different periods during the year. You need to implement the Azure SQL Database elastic pool to minimize cost. Which option or options should you configure?
a) Number of transactions only
b) eDTUs per database only
c) Number of databases only
d) CPU usage only
e) eDTUs and max data size
Answer:e

QUESTION 135

03. You are a data engineer for an Azure SQL Database. You write the following SQL statements:
CREATE TABLE Customer (
CustomerID int IDENTITY PRIMARY KEY,
GivenName varchar(100) MASKED WITH (FUNCTION = 'partial(2,"XX",0)') NULL,
SurName varchar(100) NOT NULL,
Phone varchar(12) MASKED WITH (FUNCTION = 'default()')
INSERT Customer (GivenName, SurName, Phone) VALUES ('Sammy', 'Jack', '555.111.2222');
SELECT * FROM Customer;
You need to determine what is returned by the SELECT query. What data is returned?
a) 1 SaXX Jack XXX.XXX.2222
b) 1 XXXX Jack XXX.XXX.XXXX
c) 1 xx Jack XXX.XXX.2222
d) 1 SaXX Jack xxxx
Answer:d

QUESTION 136
04. An in-house team is developing a new application. The design document specifies that data should be represented using nodes and relationships in graph structures. Individual data elements are relatively small.
You need to recommend an appropriate data storage solution. Which solution should you recommend?
a) Azure Storage Blobs
b) Cosmos DB
c) Azure Data Lake Store
d) HBase in HDInsight
Answer:b

QUESTION 137
05. Which offering provides scale-out parallel processing and dramatically accelerates performance of analytics clusters when integrated with the IBM Flash System?
a) IBM Cloud Object Storage
b) IBM Spectrum Accelerate
c) IBM Spectrum Scale
d) IBM Spectrum Connect
Answer:c

QUESTION 138
06. A company manages several on-premises Microsoft SQL Server databases. You need to migrate the databases to Microsoft Azure by using a backup process of Microsoft SQL Server. Which data technology should you use?
a) Azure SQL Database single database
b) Azure SQL Data Warehouse
c) Azure Cosmos DB
d) Azure SQL Database Managed Instance
e) HDInsight Spark cluster
Answer:d

QUESTION 139

07. A company has an Azure SQL data warehouse. They want to use PolyBase to retrieve data from an Azure Blob storage account and ingest into the Azure SQL data warehouse. The files are stored in parquet format. The data needs to be loaded into a table called lead2pass_sales.
Which of the following actions need to be performed to implement this requirement?
(Choose 4)
a) Create an external file format that would map to the parquet-based files
b) Load the data into a staging table
c) Create an external table called lead2pass_sales_details
d) Create an external data source for the Azure Blob storage account
e) Create a master key on the database
f) Configure Polybase to use the Azure Blob storage account
Answer: b, c, d,e

QUESTION 140

08. The data engineering team manages Azure HDInsight clusters. The team spends a large amount of time creating and destroying clusters daily because most of the data pipeline process runs in minutes.
You need to implement a solution that deploys multiple HDInsight clusters with minimal effort.
What should you implement?
a) Azure Databricks
b) Azure Traffic Manager
c) Azure Resource Manager templates
d) Ambari web user interface
Answer: c

QUESTION 141

09. You are designing a big data streaming solution. You need to choose the most appropriate resource for different scenarios. Which Azure resource should you choose?
To answer, drag the appropriate resource to each scenario. A resource may be used once, more than once, or not at all.
a) SQL Data Warehouse
Stream Analytics
b) SQL Data Warehouse
Databricks
c) Stream Analytics
Data Lake
d) loT Hub
Data Factory
Answer: a

QUESTION 142

A company purchases IoT devices to monitor manufacturing machinery. The company uses an Azure IoT Hub to communicate with the IoT devices. The company must be able to monitor the devices in real-time.

You need to design the solution. What should you recommend?
a) Azure Data Factory instance using Azure Portal
b) Azure Analysis Services using Microsoft Visual Studio
c) Azure Stream Analytics Edge application using Microsoft Visual Studio
d) Azure Data Factory instance using Microsoft Visual Studio
Answer: c

QUESTION 143
You are working on Azure Data Lake Store Gen1. Suddenly, you realize the need to know the schema of the external data. Which of the following plug-in would you use to know the external data schema?
A. Ipv4_lookup
B. Mysql_request
C. Pivot
D. Narrow
E. infer_storage_schema
Answer: E

QUESTION 144
You work in Azure Synapse Analytics dedicated SQL pool that has a table titled Pilots. Now you want to restrict the user access in such a way that users in 'IndianAnalyst' role can see only the pilots from India. Which of the following would you add to the solution?
A. Table partitions
B. Encryption
C. Column-Level security
D. Row-level security
E. Data Masking
Answer: D

QUESTION 145
While working on the project, you realize that the delta table is not correct. One of your friends suggests deleting the whole directory of the table and creating a new table on the same path. Would you follow the suggested solution?
A. Yes
B. No
Answer: B

QUESTION 146
Data Cleansing in Data Quality Services (DQS) includes a 2-step process for data cleansing: computer-assisted and interactive cleansing. Depending upon the computer-assisted cleansing process, during the interactive cleansing, DQS gives the data steward with information that is needed to make a decision about modifying or changing the data. For this purpose, DQS classifies the data into 5 tabs. From the below-given option, choose the tab that is not among these tabs.
A. Invalid
B. Valid
C. Suggested

D. New
E. Correct
F. Corrected
Answer: B

QUESTION 147
You need to design an enterprise data warehouse in Azure SQL Database with a table titled customers. You need to ensure that the customer supportive staff can identify the customers by matching the few characters of their email addresses but the full email addresses of the customers should not be visible to them. Which of the following would you include in the solution?
A. Row-level security
B. Encryption
C. Column Level Security
D. Dynamic Data Masking
E. Any of the above can be used
Answer: D

QUESTION 148
You need to create a quick object in a test environment and therefore you decide to create a temporal table with an "anonymous" history table. From the given below statement/remarks about the history table in this context, choose the statement(s) that is/are true.
A. You need to manually create the anonymous history table and provide its specific schema
B. The history table is created as a rowstore table
C. The history table is created as a columnstore table
D. A default clustered index is developed for the history table
E. A history table is always uncompressed. No compression is ever applied on the history table
Answer: B and D

QUESTION 149
There are a number of various analytical data stores that use different languages, models, and provide different capabilities. Which of the following is a low-latency NoSQL data store that provides a high-performance and flexible option to query structured and semi-structured data?
A. Azure Synapse Analytics
B. HBase
C. Spark SQL
D. Hive
E. None of these
Answer: B

QUESTION 150
You work in an Azure Transformational Logics (ATL) company and you have been given the responsibility to create and update query-optimization statistics utilizing the Synapse SQL resources in a dedicated SQL pool. The following are the guiding principles recommended for updating the statistics during the load process. Which of the following is/are not true?
A. Ensure that every loaded table is having at least 1 statistics object updated
B. Focus on the columns participating in ORDER BY, GROUP BY, JOIN and DISTINCT clauses

C. Update "ascending key" columns like order dates more frequently as these values are not considered/included in the statistics histogram
D. Update static distribution columns more frequently
E. None of these
Answer: D

QUESTION 151
There are a number of different options for data serving storage in Azure. These options vary based on the capability they offer. Which of the below-given options don't offer Row-Level security?
A. SQL Database
B. Azure Data Explorer
C. HBase/Phoenix on HDInsight
D. Hive LLAP on HDInsight
E. Azure Analysis Services
F. Cosmos DB
Answer:B and F

QUESTION 152
When you implement the Clean Missing Data module to a set of data, the Minimum missing value ratio and Maximum missing value ratio are two important factors in replacing the missing values. If the Maximum missing value is set to 1, what does it mean?
A. missing values are cleaned only when 100% of the values in the column are missing
B. missing values are cleaned even if there is only one missing value
C. missing values are cleaned only when there is only one missing value
D. missing values won't be cleaned
E. missing values are cleaned even if 100% of the values in the column are missing
Answer: E

QUESTION 153
On each file upload, Batch writes 2 log files to the compute node. These log files can be examined to know more about a specific failure. These two files are:
A. fileuploadin.txt and fileuploaderr.txt
B. fileuploadout.txt and fileuploadin.txt
C. fileuploadout.txt and fileuploaderr.txt
D. fileuploadout.JSON and fileuploaderr.JSON
E. fileupload.txt and fileuploadout.txt
Answer: C

QUESTION 154
You have been assigned the task to manage the storage of consumers profiles and Sales data. A general request is to create a list of "the top 100 consumers including name, account number and sales around for a specific time period" or "who are the consumers within a particular geographic region?"
Is Azure Blob storage a recommended choice for this data?
A. Yes
B. No

Answer: B

QUESTION 155

A famous online payment gateway provider is creating a new product where the users can pay their credit card bills and earn reward coins. As part of compliance, they need to ensure that all the data, including credit card details and PIIs, are securely kept. This product is backed by a dedicated SQL pool in azure Synapse analytics. The major concern is that the database team that performs maintenance should not be able to view the customer's info. Which of the following can be the best solution?

A. Implement Transparent data encryption
B. Use Azure Defender for SQL
C. Use Dynamic data masking (DDM)
D. Assign only SQL security manager role to maintenance team members

Answer: C

QUESTION 156

You have a Serverless SQL pool development assigned by your company. This should follow the best practices and optimized solutions. Which of the following solutions will help you increase the performance?

A. Use the same region for Azure Storage account and serverless SQL pool
B. Convert CSV to Parquet
C. Use CETAS
D. Use azure storage throttling

Answer: A, B and C

QUESTION 157

You have a traditional data warehouse storage with a snowflake schema with row-oriented storage that takes considerable time and low performance during queries. You plan to use clustered columnstore indexing. Will it improve query performance?

A. Yes
B. No

Answer: A

QUESTION 158

A famous fintech startup is setting up its data solution using Azure Synapse analytics. As part of compliance, the company has decided that only the finance managers should be able to see the Bank Account Number and not anyone else. Which of the following is best suited in this scenario?

A. Firewall rules to block IP
B. Row-level security
C. Column-level security
D. Azure RBAC role

Answer: C

QUESTION 159

A famous IOT devices company collects the metadata about its sensors in the field in reference data. Which of the following services can be used as input for this type of data?

A. Azure SQL
B. Blob Storage
C. Azure Event Hub
D. Azure IOT hub
Answer: A and B

QUESTION 160
You have an Azure Data Factory with Self Hosted Runtime Integration Runtime (SHIR) set up on Azure VM. During a regional failure/disaster, what is your best option for Data redundancy?
A. Utilize Microsoft managed Regional Failover by Azure Data factory
B. Use Azure Site Recovery for VM failover
C. Data is by default replicated to the paired region for Azure VM and does automatic failover
D. Utilize automatic Regional Failover for Azure VM
Answer: B

QUESTION 161
Bryan is executing an init script which is required to run a bootstrap script during the Databricks Spark driver or worker node startup.
Which kind of init script can he choose?
A. Global
B. Job
C. Cluster-scoped
D. None of the above
Answer: C

QUESTION162
The Complex event processing streaming solution which Jeffrey is working on the IoT platform, is a hybrid cloud platform where few data sources are transformed into on-premises Big Data platform. The on-premises data center and Azure services are connected via a virtual network gateway.
What kind of resources can he choose for this on-premises Big data platform connected to Azure via virtual network gateway, complex data processing and execution UDF jobs on java?
A. Spark Structured Streaming / Apache Storm
B. Apache Ignite
C. Apache Airflow
D. Apache Kafka
E. None of the above
Answer: A

QUESTION 163
Nicole is working on migrating on-premises SQL Server databases to Azure SQL data warehouse (Synapse dedicated SQL pools) tables. The tables of the dedicated SQL pools of Synapse Analytics require partition. She's designing SQL table partitions for this data migration to the Azure Synapse. The partition of the tables already contains the data, and she's looking for the most efficient method to split the partitions in the dedicated SQL pool tables.
What T-SQL statement can she use for splitting partitions that contain data?

A. CTAS
B. CETAS
C. OPENROWSET
D. Clustered Columnstore Indexes
Answer: A

QUESTION 164
Which of the following five kinds of log types can Phil select for storing Databricks Diagnostic logs?
A. Secrets
B. RDP
C. Network
D. DBFS
E. Keys
F. SQL permissions
G. Accounts
H. Spark
I. Ssh
J. Ambari
Answer: A, D, F, G and I

QUESTION 165
You are working in a cloud company and you have been assigned the responsibility of building an enterprise data lake on Azure and accomplishing big data analytics. Which of the following Azure services would you use in this scenario?
A. Azure Files
B. Azure Blobs
C. Azure Disks
D. Azure Queues
E. Azure Tables
Answer: B

QUESTION 166
You are implementing an Azure Data Lake Gen2 storage account. You need to ensure that data will be accessible for write and read operations both even if an entire data center (zonal or non-zonal) becomes unavailable. Which kind of replication would you use for the storage account? (Choose the solution with minimum cost)
A. Locally-redundant storage (LRS)
B. Zone-redundant storage (ZRS)
C. Geo-redundant storage (GRS)
D. Geo-zone-redundant storage (GZRS)
Answer: B

QUESTION 167
While working on one of your company's projects, your teammate wants to check the options for input to an Azure Stream Analytics task that needs high throughput and low latencies. He is

confused about the input that he should use in this case. He approaches you and asks you to help him. Which of the following Azure product would you suggest to him?
A. Azure Table Storage
B. Azure Blob Storage
C. Azure Queue Storage
D. Azure Event Hubs
E. Azure IoT Hub
Answer: D

QUESTION 168
You work in Azure Synapse Analytics' dedicated SQL pool that has a table titled Pilots. Now you want to restrict the user access in such a way that users in the 'IndianAnalyst' role can see only the pilots from India. Which of the following would you add to the solution?
A. Table partitions
B. Encryption
C. Column-Level security
D. Row-level security
E. Data Masking
Answer: D

QUESTION 169
You are considering deploying an Azure Databricks interactive cluster. You need to ensure that the cluster configuration is kept, even if the cluster is inactive for more than 30 days.
How would you achieve this goal?
A. Terminate the cluster manually
B. Clone the cluster after termination
C. Pin the cluster
D. Start the cluster manually
Answer: C

QUESTION 170
You are designing a big data analytics solution that will use azure stream analytics to analyze real-time Twitter data with hashtag #cloud. Which windowing function would you recommend to be used in your query, if you need to give every 5 seconds the count of tweets over the last 10 seconds?
A. Session window
B. Sliding window
C. Tumbling window
D. Hopping window
Answer: D

QUESTION 171
You have created a data frame. But before issuing SQL Queries, you decide to save your DataFrame as a temporary view. Which of the following DataFrame method will help you in creating the temporary view?
A. createTempView
B. createOrReplaceTempView

C. ReplaceTempView
D. createTempViewForDataFrame
E. CreateorReplaceDFTempView
Answer: B

QUESTION 172
While copying a Data Factory pipeline, you get a "DelimitedTextMoreColumnsThanDefined" error. What might be the possible cause behind this error? (Choose the best possible option)
A. You have reached the capacity limit of integration runtime.
B. The folder you are copying has files with different schemas.
C. Browser cache issue.
D. You have invoked REST API in Web activity.
Answer: B

QUESTION 173
What is the recommended storage format to use with Spark?
1) JSON
2) XML
3) Apache Parquet
Answer: 3

QUESTION 174
You have an Azure Data Lake Storage Gen2 container that contains 200 TB of data. Which type of data redundancy should you use to ensure that the data in the container is available for read workloads in a secondary region if an outage occurs in the primary region. The solution must minimize costs.
A. locally-redundant storage (LRS)
B. read-access geo-redundant storage (RA-GRS)
C. zone-redundant storage (ZRS)
D. geo-redundant storage (GRS)
Answer: B

QUESTION 175
You build a data warehouse in a Synapse Analytics dedicated SQL pool. Analysts write a complex SELECT query that contains multiple JOIN and CASE statements to Manipulate data for use in inventory reports.
You need to implement a solution to make the dataset available for the reports that need to be published daily. What should you implement so the solution must minimize query times.?
A. result set caching
B. a replicated table
C. an ordered clustered columnstore index
D. a materialized view
Answer: D

QUESTION 176

You are designing a dimension table for a data warehouse. Which type of slowly changing dimension (SCD) should you use for the table will track the value of the dimension attributes over time and preserve the history of the data by adding new rows as the data changes?
A. Type 1
B. Type 2
C. Type 3
D. Type 6
Answer: B

QUESTION 177
You need to trigger an Azure Data Factory pipeline when a file arrives in an Azure Data Lake Storage Gen2 container.
Which resource provider should you enable?
A. Microsoft Sql
B. Microsoft Event Grid
C. Microsoft Automation
D. Microsoft Event Hub
Answer: D

QUESTION 178
You plan to perform batch processing in Azure Databricks once daily. Which type of Databricks cluster should you use?
A. Interactive
B. High Concurrency
C. Automated
Answer: C

QUESTION 179
You have an Azure Data Factory that contains 10 pipelines. You need to label each pipeline with its main purpose of either ingesting, transforming, or loading. The labels must be available for grouping and filtering when using the monitoring experience in Data Factory.
What should you add to each pipeline?
A. an annotation
B. a correlation ID
C. a resource tag
D. a run group ID
Answer: A

QUESTION 180
What should you recommend for designing a statistical analysis solution that will use custom proprietary Python functions on near real-time data from Azure Event Hubs.
Answer:
A. Databricks
B. Synapse Analytics
C. Stream Analytics
D. Sql Database

Answer: A

QUESTION 181
You create an Azure Databricks cluster and specify an additional library to install.
When you attempt to load the library to a notebook, the library is not found.
What should you review to identify the cause of the issue?
A. global init scripts logs
B. workspace logs
C. notebook logs
D. cluster event logs
Answer: D

ONLINE RESOURCES

Practice Paper
Link : https://forms.gle/ygpuBKVwn6cGWvoQ6

QR Code :

Video Content
Link : https://www.youtube.com/playlist?list=PLzlh_31VWEFp3XTNqoS60UAOzl8NVG-5z

QR Code :

Chapter 3: Viva Voce Questions

Q 1: What is Azure Data Factory?
Answer: Azure Data Factory is a cloud-based data integration service that allows you to create, schedule, and orchestrate your data workflows.
Q 2: Explain data integration in Azure Data Factory.
Answer: Data integration in Azure Data Factory involves combining data from different sources, transforming it, and loading it into a destination data store for analytics.
Q 3: What is Azure Synapse Analytics?
Answer: Azure Synapse Analytics is an integrated analytics service that accelerates time to insight across data warehouses and big data systems.
Q 4: How does Azure Databricks support data engineering?
Answer: Azure Databricks provides a collaborative Apache Spark-based analytics platform optimized for Azure, designed to process large sets of data.
Q 5: What role does Azure HDInsight play in data engineering?
Answer: Azure HDInsight is a cloud service for processing big data, supporting open-source frameworks such as Hadoop, Spark, and Kafka.
Q 6: Describe the functionality of Azure Stream Analytics.
Answer: Azure Stream Analytics is a real-time analytics and complex event-processing engine that is designed to analyze and process high volumes of fast streaming data from multiple sources simultaneously.
Q 7: What is Azure Data Lake Storage?
Answer: Azure Data Lake Storage is a scalable and secure data lake for high-performance analytics workloads with a file system that supports big data analytics.
Q 8: How do you implement security in data solutions in Azure?
Answer: Implementing security involves using Azure Active Directory for authentication, securing data transfer with encryption, and controlling access with role-based access control.
Q 9: What is Cosmos DB and its use in data engineering?
Answer: Cosmos DB is Azure's NoSQL database that is globally distributed, multi-model, and supports schema-less data, which makes it ideal for modern data applications requiring a fast and flexible database.
Q 10: Explain how Azure Data Share works.
Answer: Azure Data Share allows sharing of data across Azure subscription boundaries, enabling organizations to easily share data with their own departments or with external organizations.
Q 11: What are data partitions in Azure Synapse Analytics?
Answer: Data partitions in Azure Synapse Analytics refer to the division of data into subsets to improve query performance and to manage data more efficiently.
Q 12: How does Azure manage the lifecycle of data?
Answer: Azure manages the data lifecycle using policies in Azure Data Factory or Azure Blob Storage that automate data archiving, retention, and deletion processes.
Q 13: What are the best practices for data loading in Azure Data Factory?
Answer: Best practices include using PolyBase for bulk data loads, optimizing data formats and structures, and managing data ingestion windows effectively.
Q 14: Describe incremental data loading in Azure.
Answer: Incremental data loading refers to the process of loading only new or changed data since the last data load, optimizing the data refresh process and minimizing resource consumption.

Q 15: How do you optimize data storage in Azure Data Lake?
Answer: Optimization can be achieved by organizing data into hierarchical namespaces, partitioning files, and compressing data to improve read/write efficiency.
Q 16: What is the role of Azure Monitor in data engineering?
Answer: Azure Monitor is used to collect, analyze, and act on telemetry data from Azure and on-premises environments, helping to maintain performance and availability of applications.
Q 17: How do you handle schema drift in Azure Data Factory?
Answer: Schema drift can be managed by enabling schema drift detection features in data flows within Azure Data Factory, which automatically identifies and handles changes in schema.
Q 18: What is the significance of data modeling in Azure Synapse Analytics?
Answer: Data modeling is crucial for organizing data in ways that support efficient data analysis and reporting in Azure Synapse Analytics.
Q 19: How does Azure ensure data recovery and backup?
Answer: Azure ensures data recovery and backup using Azure Backup and Azure Site Recovery services, providing reliable data protection and disaster recovery capabilities.
Q 20: What are Azure Data Bricks clusters?
Answer: Azure Databricks clusters are groups of compute resources in Azure Databricks where you can run your data engineering, data science, and data analytics workloads.

YouTube Link for Viva Voce Questions:
https://www.youtube.com/playlist?list=PLzlh_31VWEFqf-oMyJY3Gd93mcFc9eRPx

QR Code:

YouTube Videos Playlists for all Microsoft Certifications Videos

Microsoft Azure AI Fundamentals AZ-900
Link: https://www.youtube.com/playlist?list=PLzlh_31VWEFq9KU8Gr0ISbfj-TW6k17f8

QR Code:

Microsoft Azure Administrator AZ-104 Microsoft Azure Virtual Desktop AZ-140
Link: https://www.youtube.com/playlist?list=PLzlh_31VWEFq7JHJMuPJZcw-XShaPrUYP

QR Code:

Microsoft Azure Virtual Desktop AZ-140
Link: https://www.youtube.com/playlist?list=PLzlh_31VWEFowmPK_ro41wiljGoGKexGI

QR Code:

Microsoft Azure Developer AZ-204
Link:
https://www.youtube.com/playlist?list=PLzlh_31VWEFqT72UPVCUi6rqRqLBuwMSr

QR Code:

Designing Microsoft Azure Infrastructure Solution AZ-305
Link:
https://www.youtube.com/playlist?list=PLzlh_31VWEFpTerOknh9kgL4eTbhQwDND

QR Code:

Microsoft Azure Devops Engineer AZ-400
Link: https://www.youtube.com/playlist?list=PLzlh_31VWEFpyUIe_DuaeIkcThEfMT_BT

QR Code:

Microsoft Azure Security Engineer AZ-500
Link:
https://www.youtube.com/playlist?list=PLzlh_31VWEFqFBJgQTPNucIO0wVJdjNmS

QR Code:

Microsoft Azure Network Engineer AZ-700
Link:
https://www.youtube.com/playlist?list=PLzlh_31VWEFowujgDl16YDCvsQtmKgEqL

QR Code:

Microsoft Azure Fundamentals AZ-900
Link: https://www.youtube.com/playlist?list=PLzlh_31VWEFpeXZ2p32R1zDsgcbV8kI1K

QR Code:

Microsoft Azure Data Engineer DP-203
Link: https://www.youtube.com/playlist?list=PLzlh_31VWEFp3XTNqoS60UAOzl8NVG-5z

QR Code:

Microsoft Azure Database Administrator DP- 300
Link: https://www.youtube.com/playlist?list=PLzlh_31VWEFpv-rmc2mbpoIqUOqVW_cIo

QR Code:

9 789369 721566

Printed at Repro India Ltd.